HOW TO BE GOOD
AT DRAWING
BOOK 1

HOW TO BE GOOD
AT DRAWING
BOOK 1

Copyright © 2019 ChildrensBehaviorEducation.com
All rights reserved.
No part of this book may be reproduced
or transmitted in any form or by any means
without written permission from the author.

ISBN: 978-1-946151-05-6
1st edition

Produced by Jordan Tepper Weiner and Alexa Weiner
Illustrations by Cory Jones
Graphic Design by www.JenBrookman.com

www.ChildrensBehaviorEducation.com
261 Kimberly Rd
N. Barrington, IL 60010
Marketing@ChildrensBehaviorEducation.com
1-(313) MANNERS
1-(313) 626-6377

Table of Contents

Intro Letter 4
How To Draw Cats .... 5 & 6
How To Draw Dogs .... 7 & 8
How To Draw a Panda 9
How To Draw an Ant 10
How To Draw a Bunny 11
How To Draw a Teddy Bear 12
How To Draw a Monkey 13
How To Draw a Dolphin 14
How To Draw a Octopus 15
How To Draw a Turtle 16
How To Draw a Lion & Raccoon 17
How To Draw a Reindeer 18
How To Draw a Whale and Ram 19
How To Draw Birds 20
How To Draw a Mouse and Giraffe 21
How To Draw an Otter 22
How To Draw a Red Panda 23
How To Draw Butterflies 24
How To Draw a Dinosaur 25
How To Draw a Horse 26
How To Draw a Unicorn 27
How To Draw a Zebra 28
How To Draw a Lion 29
How To Draw a Lioness 30
How To Draw Emotions 31
Learn to Identify Anger and Pain Levels 32
Learn Important Phone Numbers 33
How To Draw Cartoon Expressions 34
How To Draw a Girl's Face .... 35 & 36
How To Draw a Boy's Face .... 37 - 39
How To Draw Hands 40
How To Draw Your Family 41
How To Draw a Park Scene 42
How To Draw Flowers 43
How To Draw a Rocket 44
Draw a Doodle Game 45
Create a Character Contest .... 46 & 47

Hi Kids,

I hope you have fun playing while learning with my How To Draw Book!

Learning how to draw will help you open a magical world of creativity and imagination!

This book provides step by step details for how to draw some of your favorite animals, sea creatures, people, faces, hands, rockets and more.

As your drawing skills grow, have fun drawing with colored pencils, crayons, chalk, charcoal, pens (there are many kinds of pens such as felt-tip or drawing pens - which are what most professionals use) and try using other materials such as paint or other media such as digital art.

Know that our how to draw illustrations are not the only way to draw - feel free to experiment and have fun creating your own drawing style! There are many other how to draw books at the library and book stores.

Quality time spent learning how to draw is a good alternative to spending to much time watching television or playing with electronics.

Drawing can help you with coping and communication skills, or just be plain fun to do!

Most importantly, have fun while learning how to draw. Understand that patience and practice are needed - the more time and effort you invest in drawing the better you drawings will be.

Polly

Draw Snowball or create your own cat!

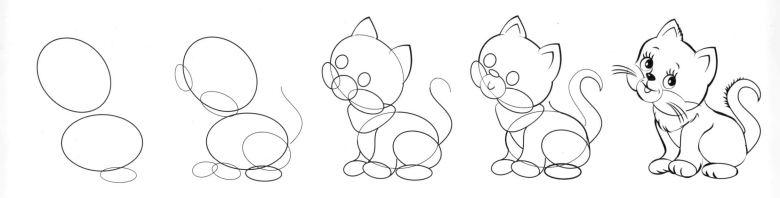

Draw Katy or create your own cat!

Draw Spot or create your own dog!

Draw Toby or create your own dog!

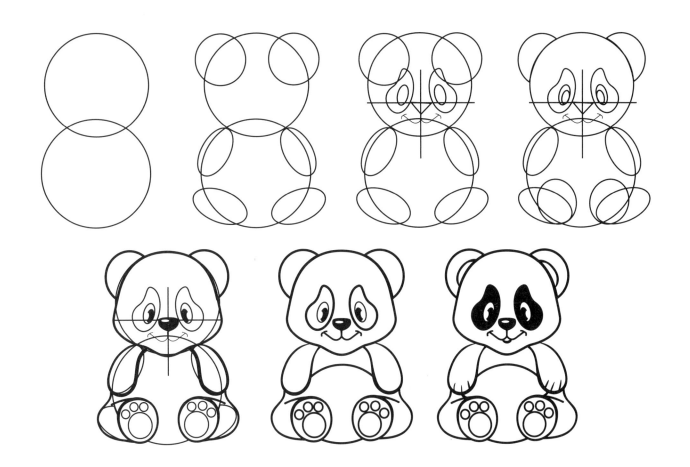

Draw Paula or create your own panda!

Draw Artimus or create your own ant!

Draw Cuddles or create your own bunny!

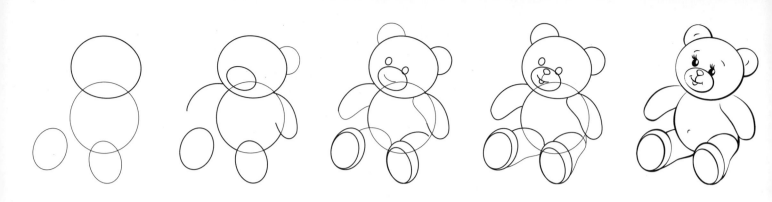

Draw Suzie or create your own teddy bear!

Draw Marty or create your own monkey!

Draw Finn or create your own dolphin!

Draw Octavia or create your own octopus!

Draw your own turtle!

16 How to Draw

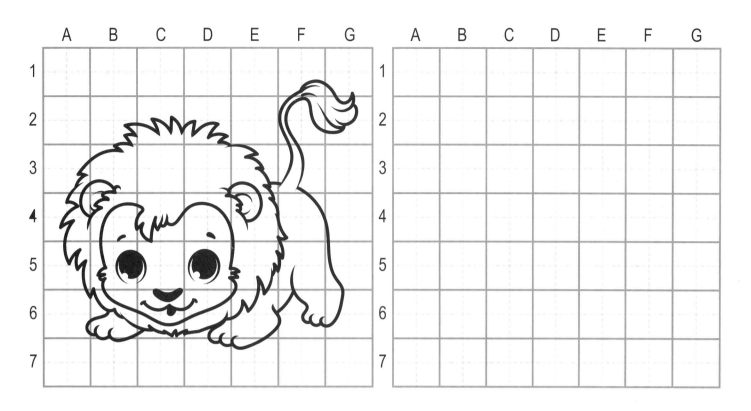

Copy the characters onto the blank grid to the right, using the grid lines to help you draw the correct sizes and shapes.

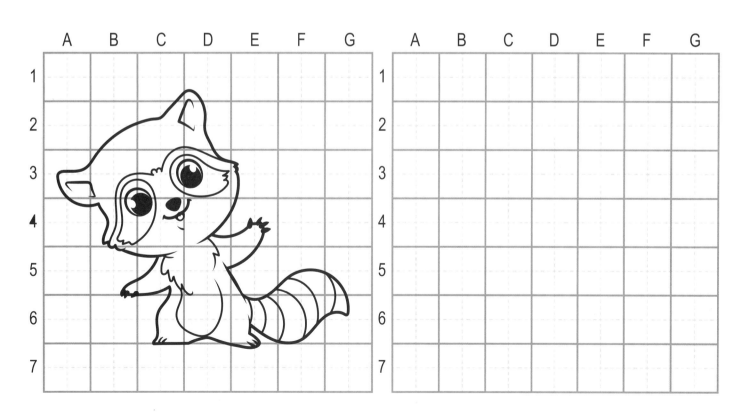

Draw Comet or create your own Reindeer!

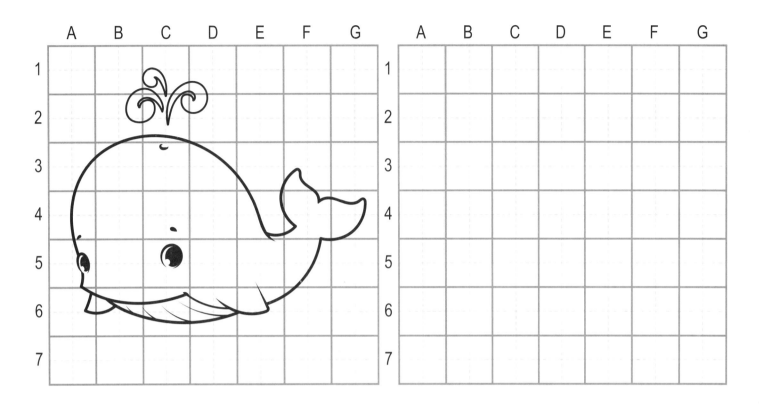

Copy the characters onto the blank grid to the right, using the grid lines to help you draw the correct sizes and shapes.

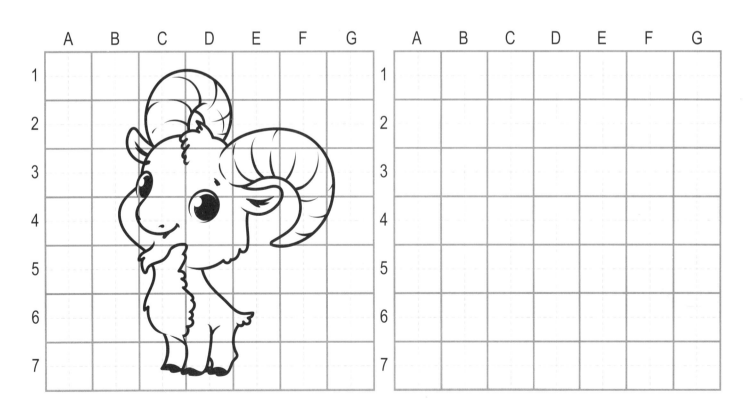

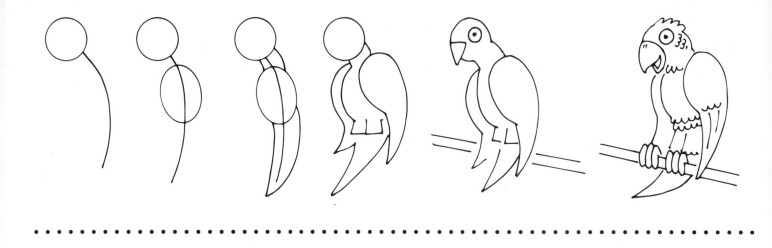

Draw Verde or Tweety or create your own birds!

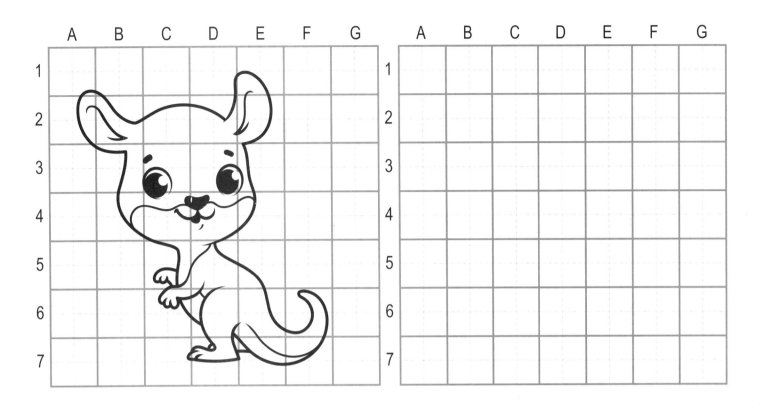

Copy the characters onto the blank grid to the right, using the grid lines to help you draw the correct sizes and shapes.

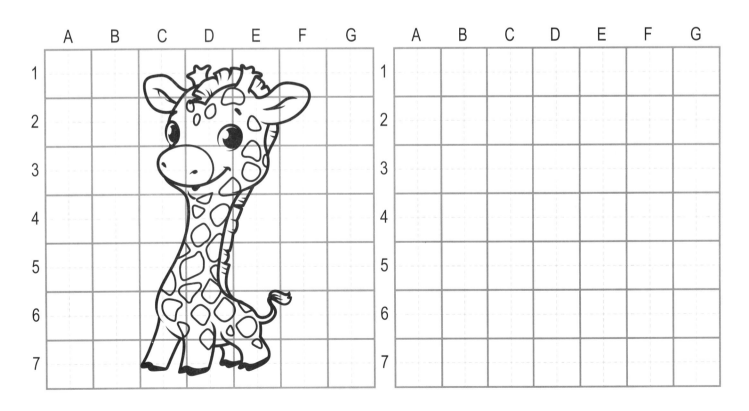

Draw Otto or create your own Otter!

Draw Rico or create your own Red Panda!

Draw these or create your own butterflies!

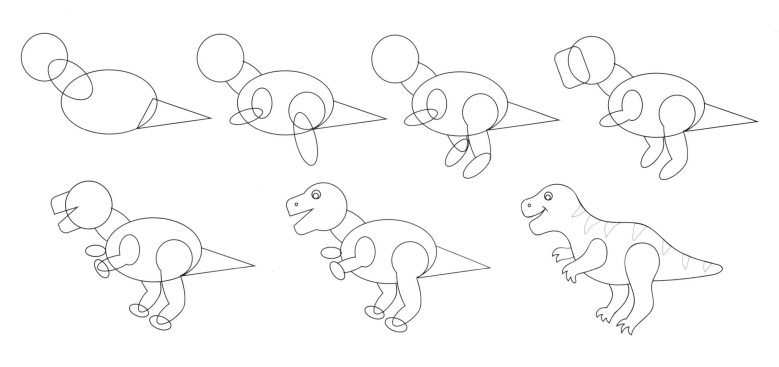

Draw Dino or create your own dinosaur!

Draw Harvey or create your own horse!

Draw Wishes or create your own unicorn!

Draw Zayda or create your own zebra!

Draw Leroy or create your own lion!

Draw Lucy or create your own lioness!

Emotions

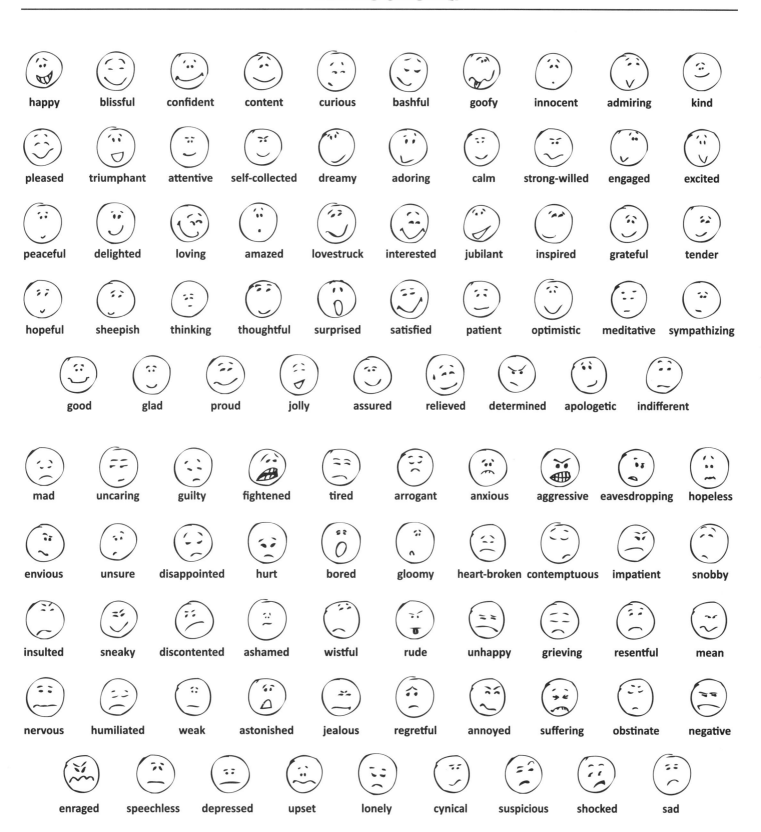

Behavior Scales help with anger and pain communication and management.
Learn to rate your anger or pain from 1 to 10. 1 being none and 10 being extreme.

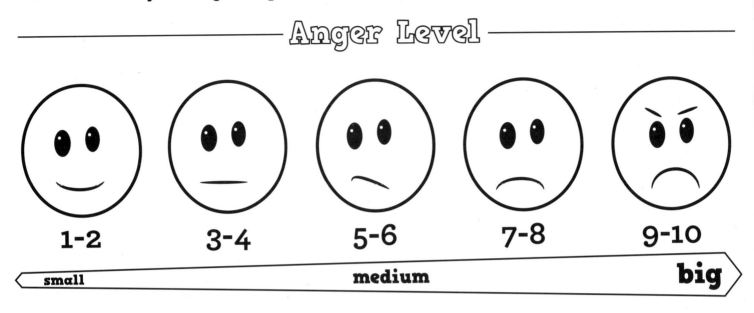

Sometimes our emotions are strong and feel big, sometimes they feel in the middle, and sometimes our emotions feel small and tiny.

We all have feelings and all feelings are OK!
Use the scale above to rate your emotion from small, medium, to big.

If you are angry, or have other big emotions,
you still need to treat others with kindness or respect.

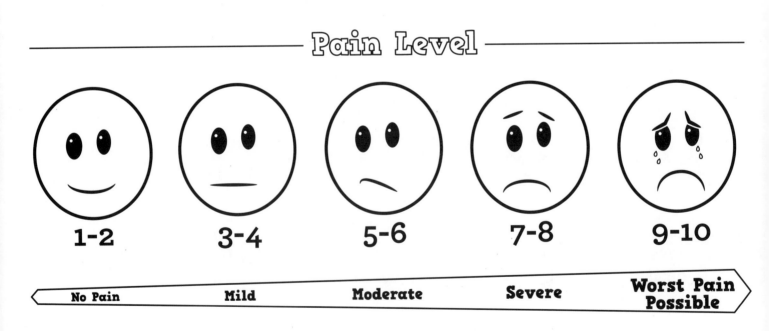

Tell a trusted adult when, why and what your anger or
pain level is when something goes wrong.

Learn to dial important phone numbers

Memorize and learn to write these phone numbers and practice dialing your parents' numbers.

MOM __ __ __   __ __ __   __ __ __ __

DAD __ __ __   __ __ __   __ __ __ __

POLICE 9 1 1

How to Draw

Draw your own cartoon expressions

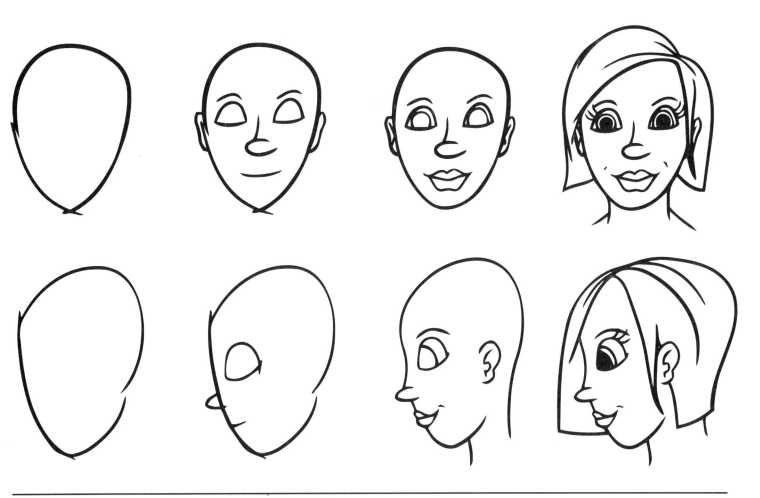

Draw a girl's face

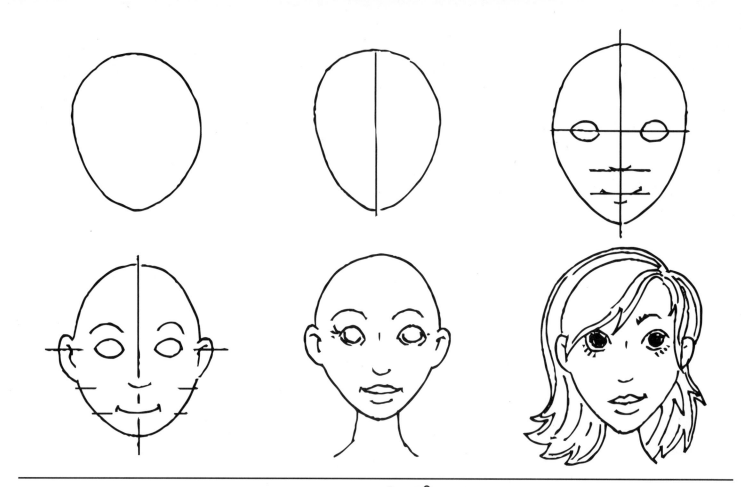

Draw a girl's face

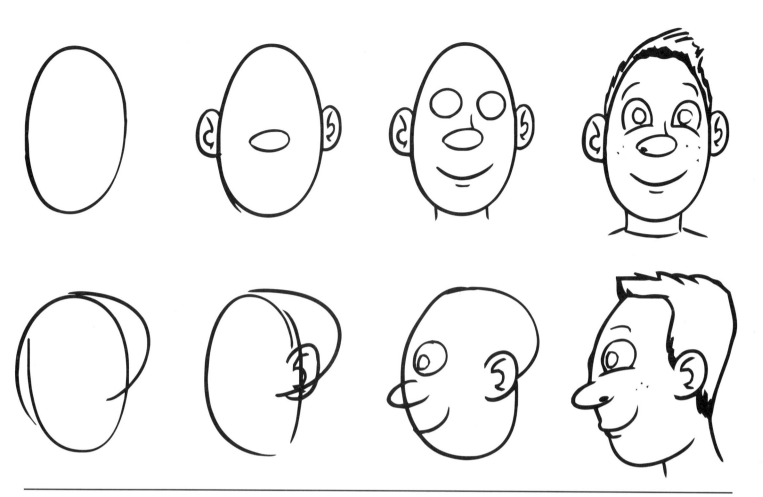

Draw a boy's face

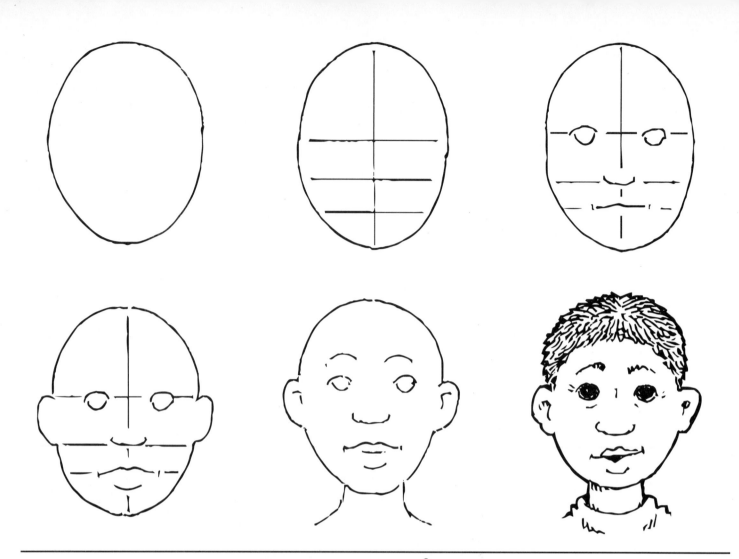

Draw a boy's face

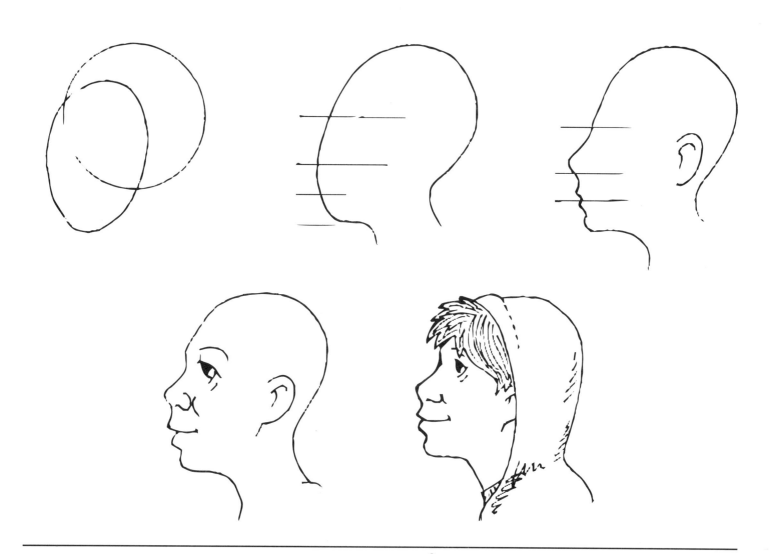

Draw a boy's face

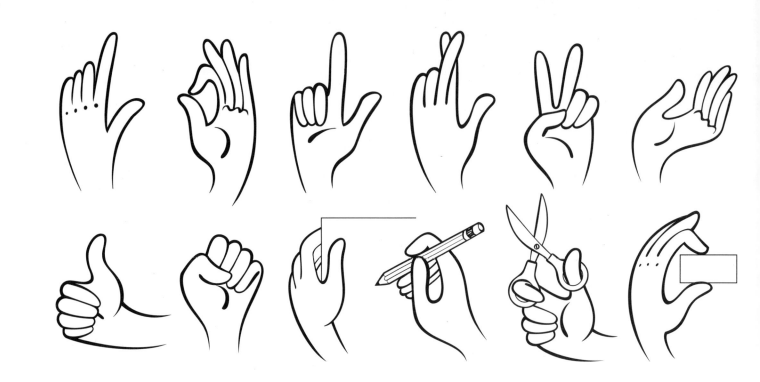

Learn to draw hands, then put them on characters

40 How to Draw

Draw your own family

Draw your own park scene

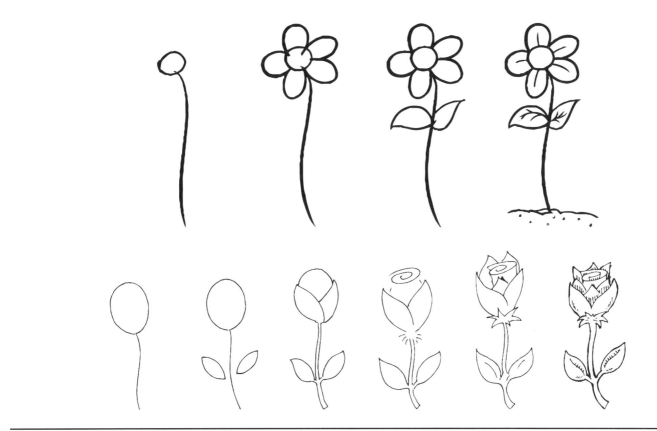

Draw flowers or create your own

Draw a rocket or create your own

DRAW A DOODLE GAME

The Doodling game is a fun creative game that helps improve drawing, thinking and imagination skills.

1 Start the game by drawing a squiggle, line, some type of mark or partial drawing on a blank sheet of paper.

2 Hand the unfinished drawing to another person playing the game.

3 The next player finishes the doodle by making it into something.

4 The person that finished the doodle begins a new game by starting a new doodle and handing it to another player.

FINISH THIS DOODLE!

How to Draw

CREATE A CHARACTER CONTEST

Enter to help build our library of character role models (animals, mythical creatures, or people).

1. Draw a picture of your character.
2. Name your character.
3. Write a short one or two phrase rhyme that describes which manner the character would like to teach.
4. Optional: Write a couple short helpful tips to help others learn the desired behavior.
5. Scan and submit your entry at **www.howtobegoodforsanta.com/contest-submission**
6. Have fun, and good luck!

Each character should appeal to children ages four through eight and should address a behavior to help build life skills and self-worth. Characters don't have to be perfectly drawn. We have professional illustrators that will help perfect great character ideas.

You can find a list of our existing characters and the behaviors they represent by visiting **www.ChildrensBehaviorEducation.com** and looking at the custom gold star reward stickers. The How To Be Good Flashcards are examples of characters, rhymes and helpful tips that are already created.

Top prizes only awarded to characters used in How To Be Good materials.

If multiple contestants submit the same character idea, the first contestant's submission will be the top prize winner. (All submissions are tracked via time/date stamp on submission.)

Everyone can be a winner, even if you are not a top prize winner, by having your character created into a custom plush animal or doll.

Each character is skillfully hand sewn by an artist and is made from safe, premium and hypoallergenic plush fabrics.

For a 10% discount on any custom plush animal or doll go to: **www.howtobegoodforsanta.com/budsies**.

Contestants waive all rights for ideas and materials submitted.

DRAW YOUR CHARACTER HERE!

Date Submitted_____ Contestant first and last name_____

Age of contestant_____ Parent first and last name_____
(If contestant is under 18)

Parent email address_____ Phone Number_____

Submit your entry at
www.howtobegoodforsanta.com/contest-submission

How to Draw

We hope you enjoyed the book.

Run through life happy and free while treating others with dignity.

**Make sure to try more
How To Be Good materials!**